SCHOLASTIC

Just-Right
Reading Response
Activity Sheets
for Young Learners

50 Reproducible Graphic Organizers That Help Children
Write Meaningful Responses to the Books They Read

Erica Bohrer

New York • Toronto • London • Auckland • Sydney
Mexico City • New Delhi • Hong Kong • Buenos Aires

Teaching *Resources*

To my mother, Maria LaPlaca Bohrer,
who has been my constant supporter,
and Mary Beth Spann,
who introduced me to the world of teachers as writers

Edited by Joan Novelli
Cover design by Maria Lilja
Interior design by Solas
Cover and interior illustrations by Teresa Anderko, Rusty Fletcher, and Mike Moran

ISBN-13: 978-0-545-13370-8
ISBN-10: 0-545-13370-X

Contents

About This Book

Just-Right Reading Response Activity Sheets for Young Learners features 50 fun, motivating, and ready-to-use comprehension-boosting graphic organizers that engage students in becoming active learners. Designed for use with fiction and nonfiction books, these graphic organizers offer a visual and concrete way for young readers to focus their thinking, organize information, and respond to literature in meaningful ways. Using the activity sheets in this book, students read with a purpose to build word knowledge, practice comprehension strategies, explore story elements, make connections, and much more.

Why Use Graphic Organizers for Reading Response?

Research has shown that graphic organizers are effective in improving comprehension. Graphic organizers provide a visual framework in which children can structure their responses to literature and relate to the "big picture" view of concepts (Beck, Omanson, & McKeown, 1982; as cited in Tompkins, 2007). The use of graphic organizers helps students organize information, activate prior knowledge, and make connections between new information (Burke, 2009). Graphic organizers are ideal for diverse learners, including English Language Learners, eliciting visual responses that allow children to demonstrate their understanding through drawings and brief written responses. With simple formats and visually appealing themes, the response activity sheets in this book go beyond fundamental graphic organizers to appeal to young learners and support success.

Getting Started

The activities in this book are designed to supplement your reading program, and lend themselves for use with the whole class, small groups, and individual students. They're also just right for sending home with students to support the reading they do outside of school. (For more information on send-home reading log folders, see page 9.) However you choose to use the materials in this book, the pages are organized in five sections for ease of selection. You may use the activities in any order to support the skills and strategies you are teaching. For an overview of each section, see pages 6–7.

Teaching Tip

Before introducing a graphic organizer to the class, test it out. Make any changes necessary to meet your instructional needs.

Emergent Literacy Skills

Many of the reading response activities provide engaging practice in emergent literacy skills, including initial sounds, rhyming words, and sight words. For example, I Spy Letters (page 21) addresses basic concepts and conventions of print, providing practice with letter recognition. Sight Word Quilt (page 22) focuses students' attention on high-frequency words, necessary for fluent reading. Use the blank sight-word quilt template (page 23) to provide practice with additional words. The Word Family House (page 24) and Word Family Tree (page 25) help students develop awareness of spelling patterns and learn to use what they know to improve reading. Children can complete these pages more than once, for repeated practice with familiar words (as with sight words or a word family) and to focus attention on new letters and words.

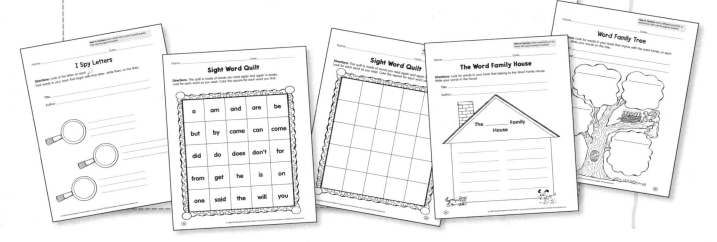

Reading Logs

(pages 15–20)

These appealing reading logs encourage children to set aside time for independent reading and provide a visual record of their reading progress. Varied response prompts on these pages invite children to notice something each time they read—from new words to characteristics of different genres.

Word Study & Vocabulary

(pages 21–29)

These activity pages support young learners in developing early reading skills, including concepts about print, letter recognition, sight-word vocabulary, and decoding strategies.

Reading Comprehension Strategies

(pages 30–47)

From making predictions to exploring story elements, these activity pages enhance comprehension with before-, during-, and after-reading activities.

Just-Right Reading Response Activity Sheets for Young Learners © 2010 by Erica Bohrer, Scholastic Teaching Resources

Personal Response

(pages 48–59)

These activity pages promote higher-level thinking skills with activities that let children analyze and evaluate the text.

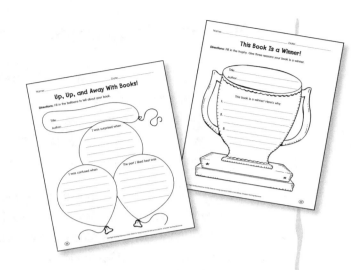

Nonfiction

(pages 60–64)

Designed for use with nonfiction texts in particular, these graphic organizers help students identify characteristics of this genre (such as common text features and graphic aids) and develop strategies (such as note-taking) for understanding and remembering important information.

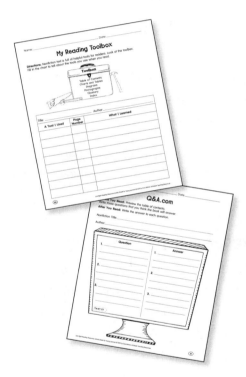

Modeling Reading Response Activity Sheets

Research shows that graphic organizers are most effective when modeled first (Bowman et al., 1998; as cited in Jacobson, 2008). The following mini-lesson provides a framework for modeling the use of any of the activity sheets in this book. In advance of this mini-lesson, prepare to enlarge the organizer for all students to easily see (for example, by creating a transparency for use with an overhead projector or by scanning to create an interactive whiteboard page). You may also give each student a copy of the organizer to follow along.

1. Read aloud a picture book that is a good match for the graphic organizer you have selected. As you read, pause to check for understanding. Be sure to ask individual and whole-class questions, such as "Who can tell us why the character acted this way?" (individual) and "Raise your hand if you agree with the way the character acted" (whole class).

2. Upon completion of the story, introduce the graphic organizer and share your rationale for using it. Complete the graphic organizer as students follow along. Use a "think-aloud" approach to help students understand your process.

3. Once students understand how to use the graphic organizer, you can assign it as an independent response activity following a second read-aloud, a guided-reading lesson, independent reading, or at-home reading.

Classroom Management and Assessment Options

For ease of use, you may wish to photocopy a class set of each of the reading response activities in this book at the beginning of the year. Place each set in a labeled file folder, and glue a copy to the front for quick identification. You may also wish to set up individual reading response folders to support students in managing these activity pages. (See reproducible Reading Folder Labels, page 13.)

The reading response activities in this book are also useful as tools to assess students' ability to follow directions, reading comprehension, and effort. Throughout the year, place reading response activities in a portfolio to document student growth.

Send-Home Reading Log Folders

According to *Reading Is Fundamental*, as little as 10 minutes of free reading a day can improve a child's reading skills and habits. Independent reading at home is an important part of any language arts program, and students are often required to keep track of their additional reading. An easy way to document children's independent reading is to create a reading log folder for each student. Setting up reading log folders will help students and their families keep track of the reading they do and provide a visual record of their success as they read together each day. To set up reading folders for students to use at home, follow these easy steps.

Materials

- ❖ Family Letter (page 14)

- ❖ Reading Folder Labels (page 13)

- ❖ Reading Logs (pages 15–20)

- ❖ File folders (or pocket folders)

- ❖ Reading response activities (pages 21–64)

1. Fill in the days on a copy of the family letter. Then copy a class supply of the letter, the reading folder labels, and the reading logs.

2. Give each student a file folder. Have students choose a label and write their name on it. Students can decorate their folders, then glue the label to the front.

3. Inside each student's folder on the left, staple a family letter. Assist students in selecting a reading log and staple that inside the folder on the right. (Modify both the letter and reading logs as needed to meet students' needs.)

4. In addition to the reading log, include other reading response activity sheets in the folder as desired. You may wish to paper clip these to the folder for security.

Helpful Hints for Success

To ensure greatest success, keep the following tips in mind when using the reading response activity sheets.

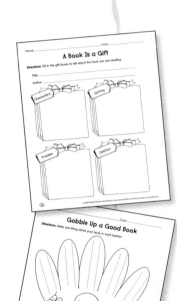

✤ Introduce the graphic organizers and model their use before expecting students to use them independently.

✤ Use one book to show students how they can complete different graphic organizers with the same text. This will give students more choice in their response activities.

✤ When sharing read-alouds with the class, look for opportunities to use graphic organizers. This will further demonstrate to students the value in using these tools and support them in transferring knowledge as they use the activity sheets on their own.

✤ Show students how to use sticky notes to mark passages in a text that they may want to refer to as they complete a reading response activity sheet.

✤ Encourage students to embellish the reading response activity sheets with decorative details. Adding a personal touch will enhance the appeal of these pages.

✤ Be open to modifications students may wish to make to the graphic organizers. For example, students may opt to complete A Book Is a Gift (page 44) by drawing pictures or using words. Either will allow for successful completion of the page. Gobble Up a Good Book (page 47) is set up to explore story elements, but students might like to use the same format to record facts from a nonfiction book. In this case, they can simply mask the labels on each feather and proceed.

Extension Activities

Consider the following suggestions to extend student learning with the activity sheets.

Same Skill, New Design: After completing an activity sheet, invite students to create a new graphic organizer design that targets the same skill. Help students refine their graphic organizers as needed, then publish them for the class to use.

A Colorful Classroom Display: Children can bring their own creative touches to the activity sheets by coloring the pages and adding details. Arranged on a bulletin board or other wall space, these reading response activity sheets make a colorful display that celebrates children's learning. This display also helps children appreciate different viewpoints.

Book Talks: Many of the graphic organizers can help students prepare for book talks—short presentations about a book they've read.

Scaffolding Skills: The reading response activity sheets in this book naturally lend themselves to scaffolding student learning. For example, the brief writing students do on the activity sheets may lead to more extensive writing based on a text. Examples follow.

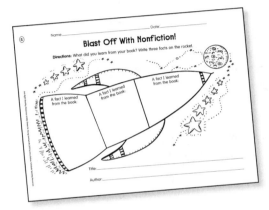

Students can use information from the sequencing reading response activity sheet Stir Up a Good Story (page 42) to assist them with writing (or telling) a book summary.

Using the facts they record on Blast Off With Nonfiction! (page 62), students can go further and write a simple research report.

Connecting Reading and Writing: Many of the same activity sheets students use for reading response are also just right for use as pre-writing graphic organizers. Students can use these pages to plan their own stories, and in the process gain understanding of how reading and writing are connected. (See example, right.)

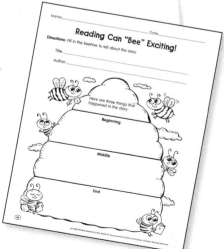

Students can use Reading Can "Bee" Exciting! (page 36) as a pre-writing graphic organizer to plan the beginning, middle, and end of a story they are writing.

Connections to the Language Arts Standards

The reading response activities in this book follow the standards for grades K–2 as outlined by the Mid-continent Regional Educational Laboratory (McREL,) an organization that collects and synthesizes national and state K–12 curriculum standards.

Uses the general skills and strategies of the reading process

❖ Understands that print conveys meaning

❖ Understands how print is organized and read

❖ Previews text (skims; uses pictures, textual clues, text format)

❖ Creates mental images from pictures and print

❖ Uses meaning clues (pictures, picture captions, title, cover, headings, story structure, story topic) to aid comprehension and make predictions about content

❖ Uses basic elements of phonetic analysis and structural analysis

❖ Understands level-appropriate sight words and vocabulary

❖ Uses self-correction strategies (searches for cues, identifies miscues, rereads, asks for help)

❖ Uses reading skills and strategies to understand and interpret a variety of literary texts

❖ Uses reading skills and strategies to understand a variety of familiar literary passages and texts (such as fairy tales, folktales, fiction, nonfiction, legends, fables, myths, poems, nursery rhymes, picture books, predictable books)

❖ Knows setting, main characters, main events, sequence, and problems in stories

❖ Makes simple inferences regarding the order of events and possible outcomes

❖ Knows the main ideas or theme of a story

❖ Relates stories to personal experiences

Uses reading skills and strategies to understand and interpret a variety of informational texts

❖ Uses reading skills and strategies to understand a variety of informational texts

❖ Understands the main idea and supporting details of simple expository information

❖ Summarizes information found in texts

❖ Relates new information to prior knowledge and experience

Source: *Content knowledge: A compendium of standards and benchmarks for K–12 education.* Mid-continent Research for Education and Learning. Online database: http://www.mcrel.org/standards-benchmarks.

Resources and References

Bowman, L.A., Carpenter. J. & Paone, R. (1998). "Using graphic organizers, cooperative learning groups, and higher order thinking skills to improve reading comprehension." M.A. Action Research Project, Saint Xavier University. Chicago.

Burke, K. (2009). *How to assess authentic learning*. Thousand Oaks, CA: Corwin.

Jacobson, J. (2008). *Reading response for fiction: Graphic organizers & mini-lessons*. New York: Scholastic.

Kendall, J. S. & Marzano, R. J. (2004). *Content knowledge: A compendium of standards and benchmarks for K–12 education*. Aurora, CO: Mid-continent Research for Education and Learning. Online database: http://www.mcrel.org/standards-benchmarks.

Reading Is Fundamental (RIF) (2008). *RIF parent guide brochure*.

Silver, R. (2003). *First graphic organizers: Reading*. New York: Scholastic.

Tompkins, G. (2007). *Literacy for the 21st century: Teaching reading and writing in prekindergarten through grade 4*. Upper Saddle River, NJ: Pearson.

Reading Folder Labels

Name _____

Name _____

Name _____

Name _____

Name _____

Name _____

Name _____

Name _____

Family Letter

Bookworm

Dear Families,

This is your child's reading folder. It will go home with your child each
_____ . Please return it with your child the
day of week

following _____ .
day of week

This reading folder contains your child's Reading Log. Your child will use the Reading Log to keep track of books he or she reads at home. Please help your child, as needed, to complete the reading log when you share a book together and when your child reads independently.

Reading with your child at home can be an enjoyable way to spend time together. It will also help your child strengthen skills in reading. Through reading, children also learn about writing and the ways authors connect ideas to tell stories or share information. Reading together is also a good way to help your child build a foundation for understanding grammar and mechanics. The more children read, the better readers and writers they become!

When you read together, be sure to take a few minutes to talk about an interesting part of the story, a new word, a favorite character, or something the story reminds you of. Making these kinds of connections can help improve your child's understanding.

I hope that reading together is a rewarding experience for both you and your child.

Sincerely,

Name: _____ Date: _____

Dig Into a Good Book

Directions: Fill in the chart each time you read.

Reading Skills
- Use the pictures.
- Think about what I know.
- Figure out new words.
- Retell the story.

Date	Title and Author	A Reading Skill I Practiced

Name: _____

Date: _____

Time to Read!

Directions: Fill in the chart each time you read.

Date	Title and Author	Time	A Thought or Question I Had
	Title: _____ Author: _____	I read for _____ minutes.	
	Title: _____ Author: _____	I read for _____ minutes.	
	Title: _____ Author: _____	I read for _____ minutes.	
	Title: _____ Author: _____	I read for _____ minutes.	
	Title: _____ Author: _____	I read for _____ minutes.	

Name: _____

Date: _____

Question of the Day

1. What would be another good title for this book?

2. What event was most important and why?

3. Why do you think the author wrote this book?

4. How do you think you are like one of the characters?

5. My Own Question: _____

Directions: Each time you read, choose a question to answer.

Date	Title	Question Number	My Response

Name: _____ Date: _____

Building With Books

Directions: Complete each "story" of this building by reading a different kind of book.

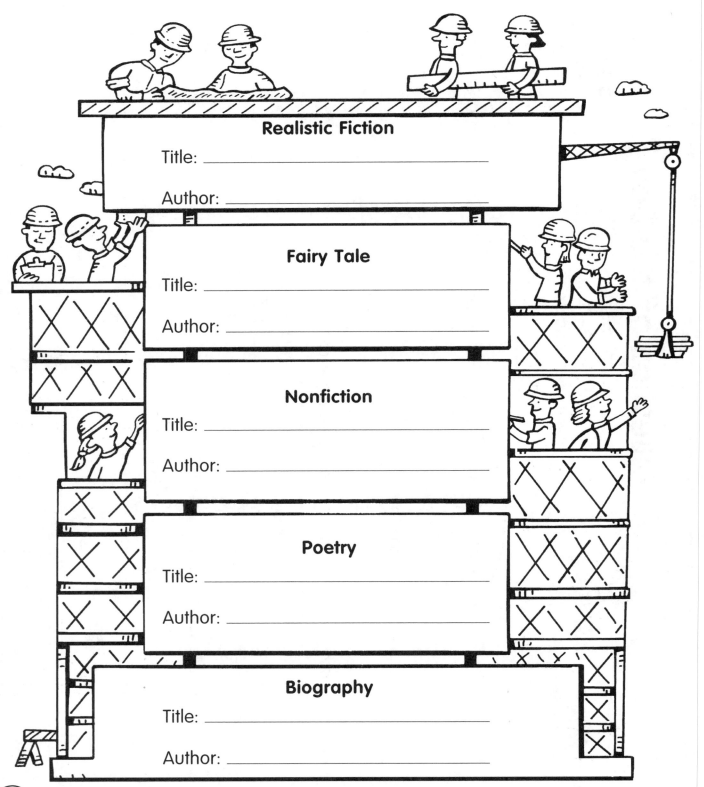

Realistic Fiction

Title: _____

Author: _____

Fairy Tale

Title: _____

Author: _____

Nonfiction

Title: _____

Author: _____

Poetry

Title: _____

Author: _____

Biography

Title: _____

Author: _____

Magic Wand Words

Directions: Look for special words in your book. Each day, fill in the magic wand number to tell about words you found. Give an example.

1 → Words that tell about a time or place

2 → Words that begin with the same sound, like "**f**ive **f**unny **f**ish"

3 → Words in **bold** or *italics* or BIG letters

4 → Words that help me use my five senses to read 👁 👂 ✋ 👃 👄

Title: _____	Author: _____	
Date	**Magic Wand Number**	**Examples of Words**
	⭐	
	⭐	
	⭐	
	⭐	
	⭐	

Name:_____   Date:_____

Chapter-Book Series Checklist

Directions: ✓ each title you read. For each book, tell something you learned about a character.

Series Title: _____

Series Author: _____

Important Characters: _____

Title	What I Learned About a Character
☐ _____	
☐ _____	
☐ _____	
☐ _____	
☐ _____	
☐ _____	

Just-Right Reading Response Activity Sheets for Young Learners © 2010 by Erica Bohrer, Scholastic Teaching Resources

Name:_____ Date:_____

I Spy Letters

Directions: Look at the letter on each ⌕.
Find words in your book that begin with that letter. Write them on the lines.

Title:_____

Author:_____

Name:_____ Date:_____

Sight Word Quilt

Directions: This quilt is made of words you read again and again in books.
Look for each word as you read. Color the square for each word you find.

a	am	and	are	be
but	by	came	can	come
did	do	does	don't	for
from	get	he	is	on
one	said	the	will	you

Name:_____ Date:_____

Sight Word Quilt

Directions: This quilt is made of words you read again and again in books. Look for each word as you read. Color the square for each word you find.

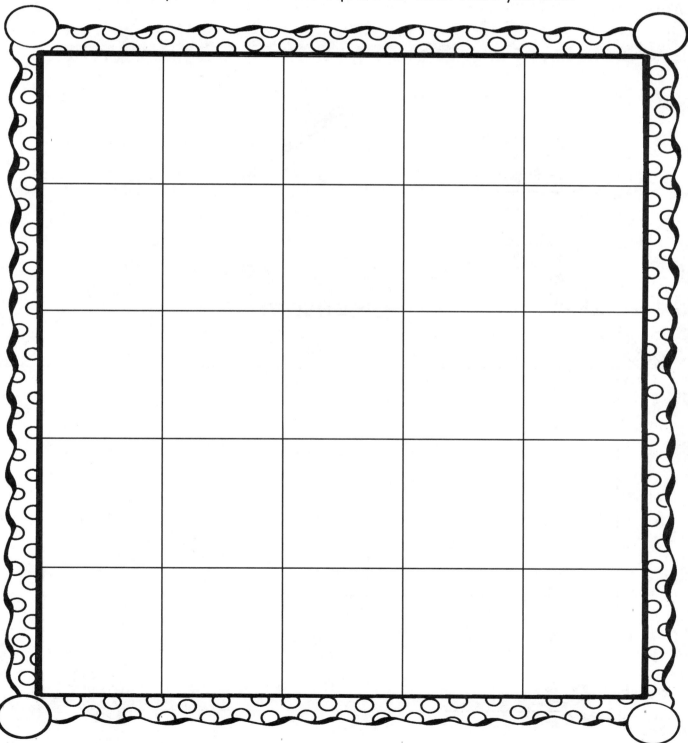

Name:_____ Date:_____

The Word Family House

Directions: Look for words in your book that belong to this Word Family House. Write your words in the house.

Title:_____

Author:_____

The _____ Family

House

Name:_____ Date:_____

Word Family Tree

Directions: Look for words in your book that rhyme with the word family on each branch. Write your words on the tree.

Title:_____

Author:_____

Name:_____   Date:_____

  # Reading for Rhymes

Directions: Look for rhyming words in a book you are reading. Write words that rhyme. Draw a picture of each word.

Title:_____

Author:_____

1. _____ rhymes with _____.

2. _____ rhymes with _____.

Name:_____ Date:_____

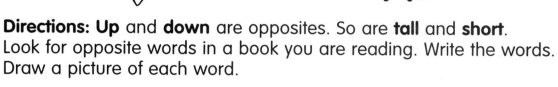  **Just the Opposite**

Directions: Up and **down** are opposites. So are **tall** and **short**.
Look for opposite words in a book you are reading. Write the words.
Draw a picture of each word.

Title:_____

Author:_____

1. _____ is the opposite of _____.

2. _____ is the opposite of _____.

Reading Is a Treasure

Directions: Look for special words when you read.
Write a word on each jewel. Color the jewels.

Title:_____

Author:_____

Name:_____ Date:_____

Weekly Words

Directions: Look for new words as you read. Write each word.
Tell what you think it means. Look at the key.
Write the number that tells how you figured it out.

Key

1 Used what I already know

2 Used a picture or text clue

3 Used a dictionary

4 Something else

Days of the Week	New Word	What I Think the Word Means	1, 2, 3, or 4?
Monday			
Tuesday			
Wednesday			
Thursday			
Friday			

Name:_____ Date:_____

Recipe for Reading

Directions: Look at the recipe card. Check the strategies you use to get ready to read. Add one new strategy to your recipe for reading!

Title:_____

Author:_____

Before Reading

☐ I look at the title and ask:
What will this book be about?

☐ I take a picture walk through the book.

☐ I make predictions about the book.

☐ I have a goal for reading.

☐ I _____
_____ .

Just-Right Reading Response Activity Sheets for Young Learners © 2010 by Erica Bohrer, Scholastic Teaching Resources

Name: _____

Take a Picture Walk

Directions: Take a picture walk before you read. Look at the pictures in the book. Draw a picture in each box to show what you learned.

Title: _____

Author: _____

Name: _____

Date: _____

On Your Mark, Get Set, Go!

Directions: Fill in the chart for a book you are reading:

K: Tell what you already know about the book's subject.

W: Tell what you learned by reading the book.

L: Tell what you still want to learn.

Title: _____

Author: _____

K	W	L

Name:_____ Date:_____

Be an "Eggs-pert" Reader!

Directions: Look at the reading strategy on each nest.
Color the chick next to each one you use with your book.
Fill in one new strategy you use to be a better reader.

Title:_____

Author:_____

I use the pictures.

I figure out new words.

I re-read when I
don't understand.

I _____

_____

_____.

Name: _____ Date: _____

Crossing the Prediction Bridge

Directions: Fill in the left side of each bridge before you read.
Fill in the right side of each bridge after you read.

Title: _____

Author: _____

Before Reading

I predict that this book
will be about

_____

_____

_____

_____ .

After Reading

This book was about

_____

_____

_____

_____ .

Before Reading

I predict that
an important character will

_____

_____

_____

_____ .

After Reading

This character

_____

_____

_____

_____ .

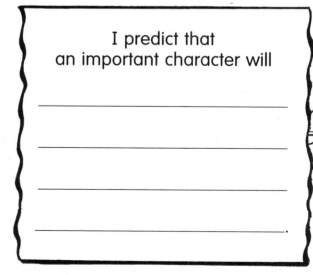

Just-Right Reading Response Activity Sheets for Young Learners © 2010 by Erica Bohrer, Scholastic Teaching Resources

Name:_____ Date:_____

Picture Detective

Directions: Look for picture clues in your book. Tell what you learned.

Title:_____

Author:_____

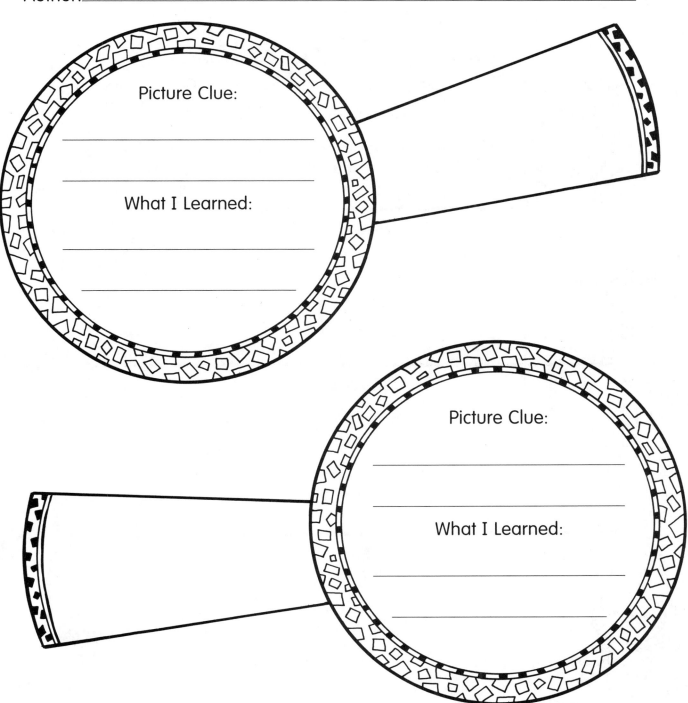

Picture Clue:

_____

_____

What I Learned:

_____

_____

Picture Clue:

_____

_____

What I Learned:

_____

_____

Name:_____ Date:_____

Reading Can "Bee" Exciting!

Directions: Fill in the beehive to tell about the story.

Title:_____

Author:_____

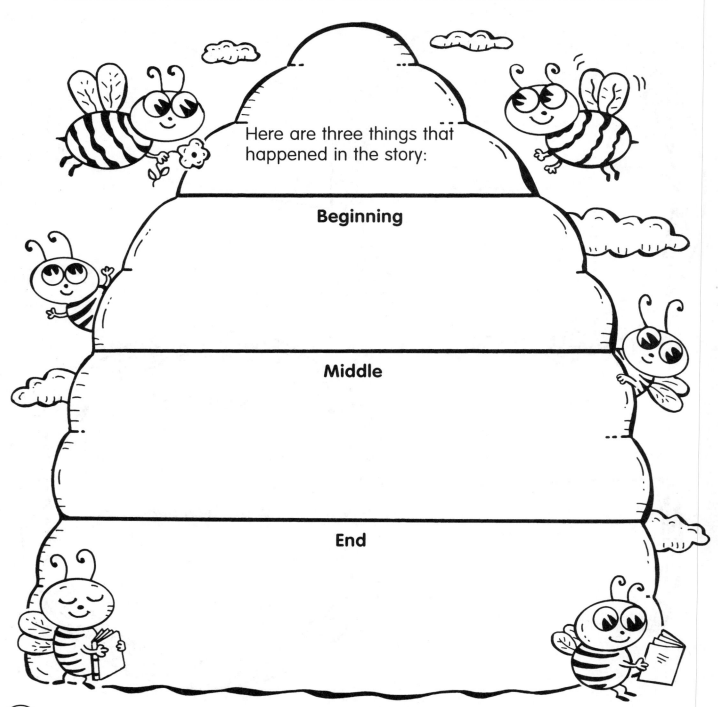

Here are three things that happened in the story:

Beginning

Middle

End

Name:_____ Date:_____

Wild About Characters

Directions: Fill in the leaves to tell about a character.

Title:_____

Author:_____

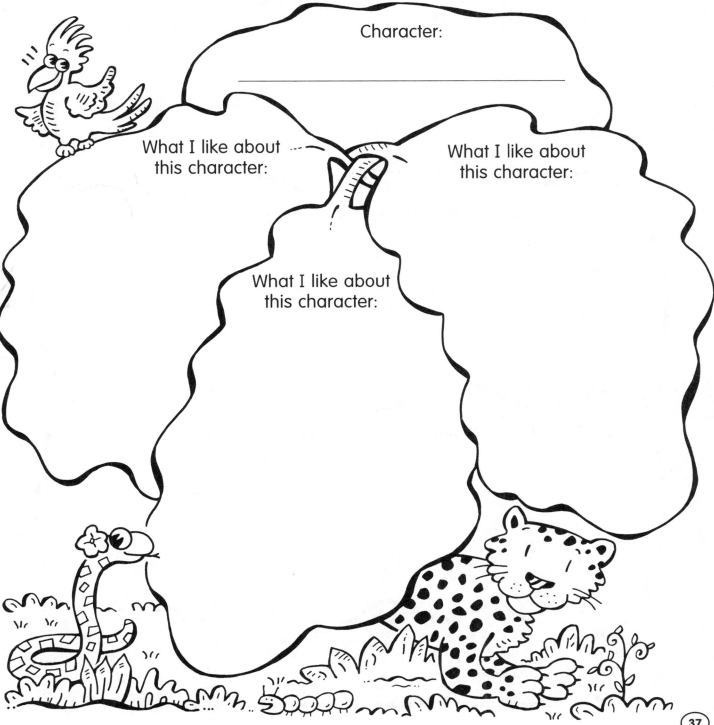

Character:

What I like about this character:

What I like about this character:

What I like about this character:

Get the Scoop on Characters

Directions: Fill in the ice-cream scoops to tell about a character.

Title:_____

Author:_____

One thing I learned about this character:

Another thing I learned about this character:

Character:_____

Name:_____ Date:_____

Who's in the News?

Directions: Fill in each section to tell about a favorite character.

EVENING EDITION ★ ★The ★Times ★ ★ ★ ★

Who?_____

Caption_____

Newsworthy Because . . .

_____

_____

_____

_____

_____

_____

_____

Also Known for . . .

Traits

Favorite Things

Other Important Information

Name:_____ Date:_____

Mirror, Mirror

Directions: Think about an important character in your book. Now think about an important event. Draw a picture in the mirror to show how the character feels about the event. Complete the sentence to explain.

Title:_____

Author:_____

Event: _____

_____

When this happens, _____ feels _____
                         (character)   (feeling)

because _____ .
                                    (reason)

Setting the Stage

Directions: Where does the story you are reading mostly happen? Draw a picture of the place. Complete the sentence to tell more.

I think the author chose this place because _____

_____

_____

_____.

Name:_____ Date:_____

Stir Up a Good Story

Directions: Think about important events in the story you are reading. Use them to retell the story. Choose words from the Word Bank to help put the events in order.

Story Events

Title:_____

Author:_____

Name:_____ Date:_____

What's the Buzz All About?

Directions: What events in your book caused a buzz? Tell about three events. Then tell which event was most important and why.

Title:_____

Author:_____

Event 1: _____

_____

_____.

Event 2: _____

_____

_____.

Event 3: _____

_____

_____.

The most important event was

_____ because _____
(1, 2, or 3?)

_____

_____

_____.

A Book Is a Gift

Directions: Fill in the gift boxes to tell about the book you are reading.

Title:_____

Author:_____

Just-Right Reading Response Activity Sheets for Young Learners © 2010 by Erica Bohrer, Scholastic Teaching Resources

Name: _____

Date: _____

Story Circles

Directions: Fill in titles of two books you have read.
Choose one idea from the Idea Bank.

Where the circles do not overlap: Tell one way each story is different.

Where the circles overlap: Tell one way the stories are alike.

Title: _____

Title: _____

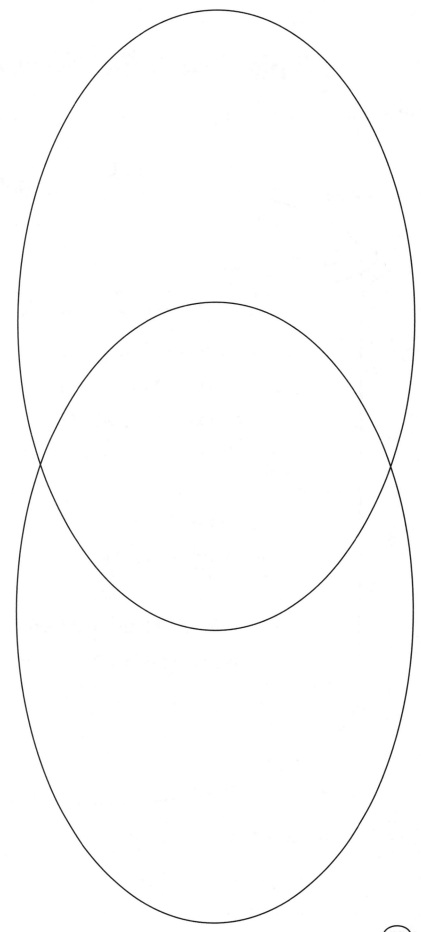

Name: _____ Date: _____

This Book Is "Stew-pendous!"

Directions: Fill in the recipe. Write the correct number on each line.

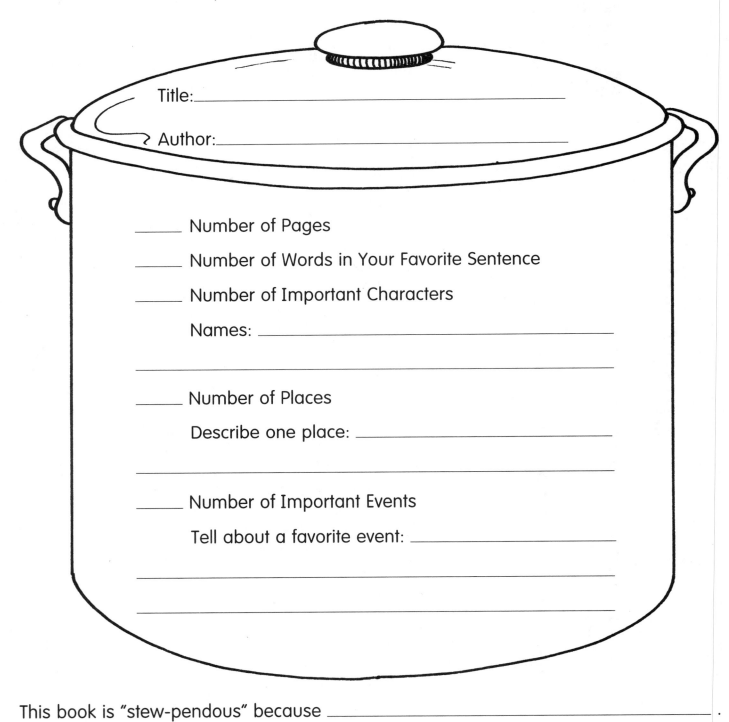

Title: _____

Author: _____

_____ Number of Pages

_____ Number of Words in Your Favorite Sentence

_____ Number of Important Characters

Names: _____

_____

_____ Number of Places

Describe one place: _____

_____

_____ Number of Important Events

Tell about a favorite event: _____

_____

This book is "stew-pendous" because _____ .

_____

Just-Right Reading Response Activity Sheets for Young Learners © 2010 by Erica Bohrer, Scholastic Teaching Resources

Name:_____ Date:_____

Gobble Up a Good Book

Directions: Write one thing about your book on each feather.

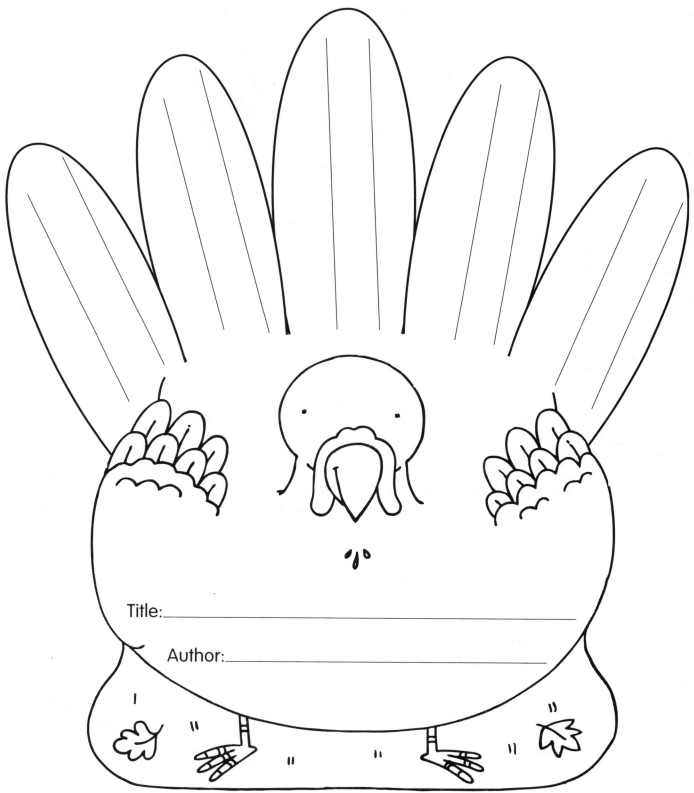

Title:_____

Author:_____

Name:_____ Date:_____

Catch the Reading Wave!

Directions: Fill in the surfboards to tell about the book that you read. Color the surfboards.

Title: _____

Why does the title fit? _____

_____

Author: _____

What did the author do best? _____

_____

What would you change if you were the author?

_____

_____

Name:_____ Date:_____

Fall Into a Good Book

Directions: Fill in the leaves to tell about the book that you read.

Title:_____

Author:_____

Write about your favorite part.

Draw a picture of your favorite part.

Name: _____

Date: _____

This Book Is the Cat's Meow!

Directions: Think about the book that you read. Fill in the comic strip.

Title: _____

Author: _____

Meow! The best thing about the beginning is
_____
_____
_____
_____
_____

Meow! The best thing about the middle is
_____
_____
_____
_____
_____

Meow! The best thing about the ending is
_____
_____
_____
_____
_____

50

Just-Right Reading Response Activity Sheets for Young Learners © 2010 by Erica Bohrer, Scholastic Teaching Resources

Name:_____ Date:_____

A Blooming Good Book

Directions: Fill in the flower to tell about your book.

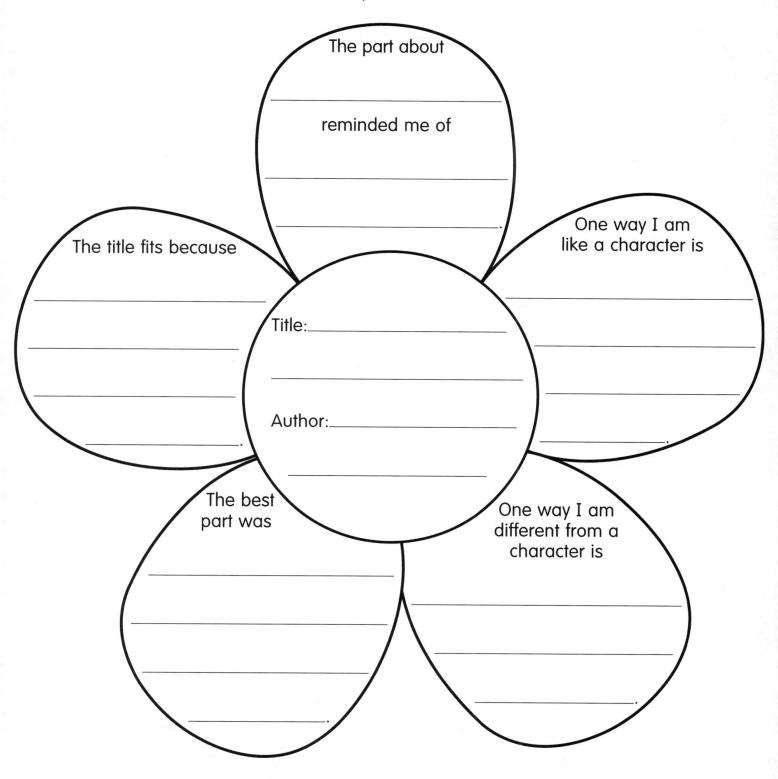

The part about
_____
reminded me of
_____.

The title fits because
_____
_____
_____.

One way I am like a character is
_____
_____
_____.

Title:_____
_____
Author:_____
_____

The best part was
_____
_____
_____.

One way I am different from a character is
_____
_____
_____.

Up, Up, and Away With Books!

Directions: Fill in the balloons to tell about your book.

Title:_____

Author:_____

I was surprised when

_____

_____

_____

I was confused when

_____

_____

_____

The part I liked best was

_____

_____

_____

Name:_____ Date:_____

 # Buggy About Books

Directions: Color in the bugs that tell about your book.

Title:_____

Author:_____

This book is fiction.

This book is nonfiction.

This book has photographs.

This book has illustrations.

This book had these new words: _____

_____

I would like to read another book by this author.

I would like to try writing like this author.

Name:_____ Date:_____

I ♡ to Read

Directions: Tell three things you love about your book.

Title:_____

Author:_____

Roses are red
Violets are blue
I love this book
And you will, too!

Here's what I love:

1._____

_____

2._____

_____

3._____

_____

_____

Just-Right Reading Response Activity Sheets for Young Learners © 2010 by Erica Bohrer, Scholastic Teaching Resources

Name:_____ Date:_____

Reading Rocks!

Directions: Complete each sentence to tell why your book rocks!

Title:_____

Author:_____

This book rocks because...

1. At the beginning _____

_____.

2. I learned these new words: _____

_____.

3. The book reminded me of _____

_____.

4. And finally... drum roll, please... _____

_____

_____.

_____.

_____.

Name:_____   Date:_____

A "Berry" Good Book!

Directions: Fill in each strawberry to tell about your book.

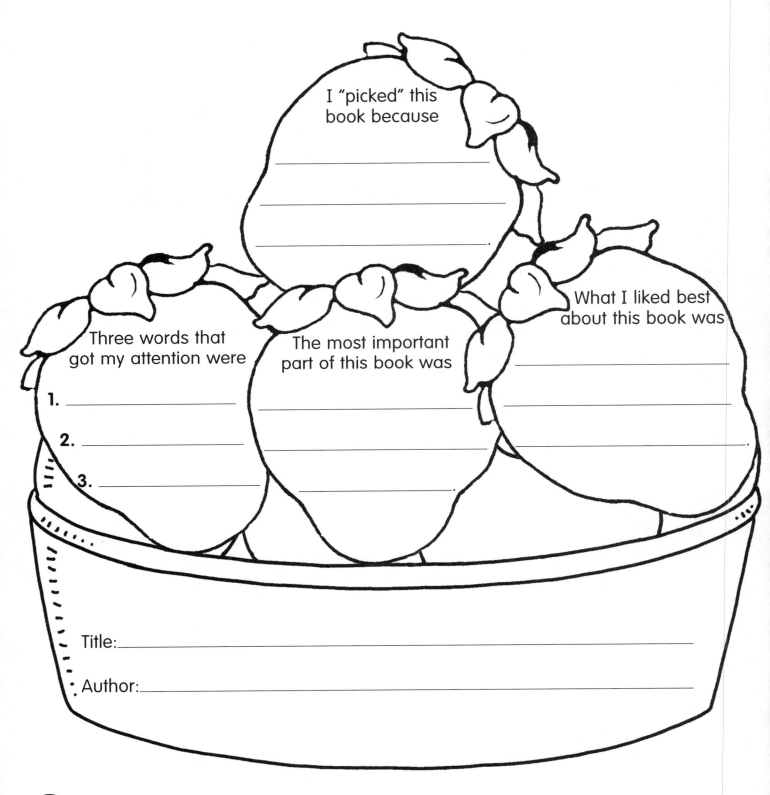

I "picked" this book because

_____

_____

_____ .

Three words that got my attention were

1. _____

2. _____

3. _____ .

The most important part of this book was

_____

_____

_____ .

What I liked best about this book was

_____

_____ .

Title:_____

Author:_____

Name:_____ Date:_____

⭐ Star Book Review ⭐

This Star Book Review brought to you _____ by _____ .
                                        (date)   (name)

I'm here to tell you about _____
                                        (book title)

by _____ .
                (author)

Summary:

This is a _____ book about _____
            (fiction or nonfiction)

_____

_____ .

Rate the Writing: ⭐1 ⭐2 ⭐3 ⭐4 ⭐5

I give the **writing** in this book _____ stars because _____
                                        (1, 2, 3, 4, or 5)

_____

_____ .

Rate the Illustrations: ⭐1 ⭐2 ⭐3 ⭐4 ⭐5

I give the **illustrations** in this book _____ stars because _____
                                              (1, 2, 3, 4, or 5)

_____

_____ .

Name: _____

Date: _____

Rainbow Reading

Directions: Fill in the rainbow to tell about the book that you read.

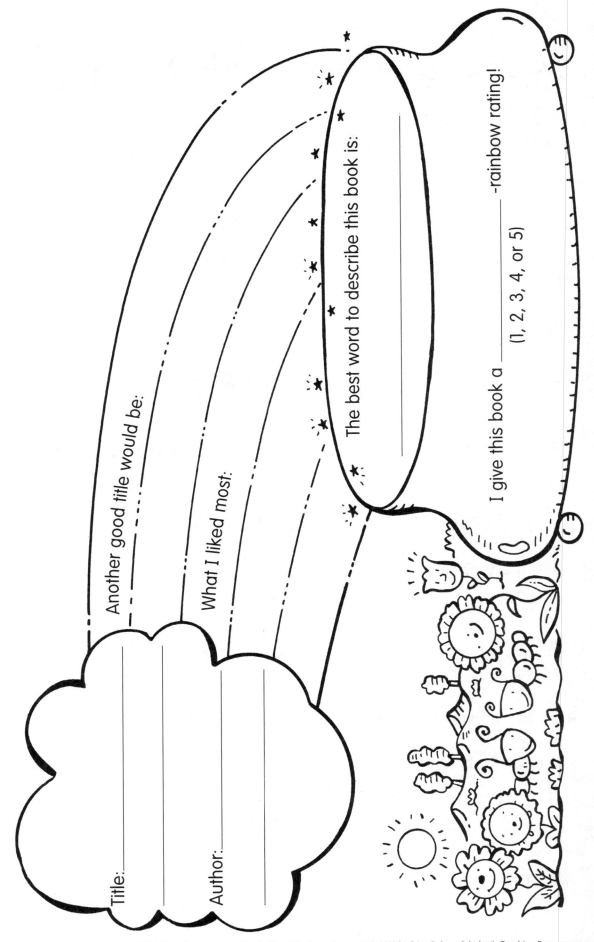

Another good title would be:

What I liked most:

The best word to describe this book is:
_____

I give this book a _____ -rainbow rating!
(1, 2, 3, 4, or 5)

Title: _____

Author: _____

Name: _____ Date: _____

This Book Is a Winner!

Directions: Fill in the trophy. Give three reasons your book is a winner.

Title: _____

Author: _____

This book is a winner! Here's why:

1. _____

_____

2. _____

_____

3. _____

_____

Name:_____ Date:_____

My Reading Toolbox

Directions: Nonfiction text is full of helpful tools for readers. Look at the toolbox. Fill in the chart to tell about the tools you use when you read.

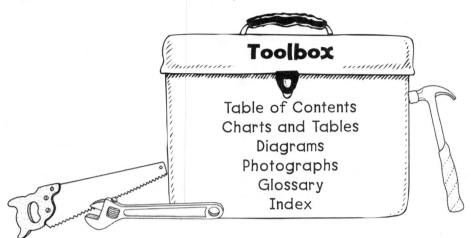

Toolbox

Table of Contents
Charts and Tables
Diagrams
Photographs
Glossary
Index

Title: _____		Author: _____
A Tool I Used	**Page Number**	**What I Learned**

Just-Right Reading Response Activity Sheets for Young Learners © 2010 by Erica Bohrer, Scholastic Teaching Resources

Name:_____ Date:_____

Q&A.com

Before You Read: Preview the table of contents.
Write three questions that you think the book will answer.

After You Read: Write the answer to each question.

Nonfiction Title:_____

Author:_____

Question	Answer
1. _____ _____ _____	1. _____ _____ _____
2. _____ _____ _____	2. _____ _____ _____
3. _____ _____ _____	3. _____ _____ _____

Search

Blast Off With Nonfiction!

Directions: What did you learn from your book? Write three facts on the rocket.

A fact I learned from the book:

A fact I learned from the book:

A fact I learned from the book:

Title: _____

Author: _____

Name:_____ Date:_____

Five-Finger Facts

Directions: What did you learn from your book? Write a fact on each finger.

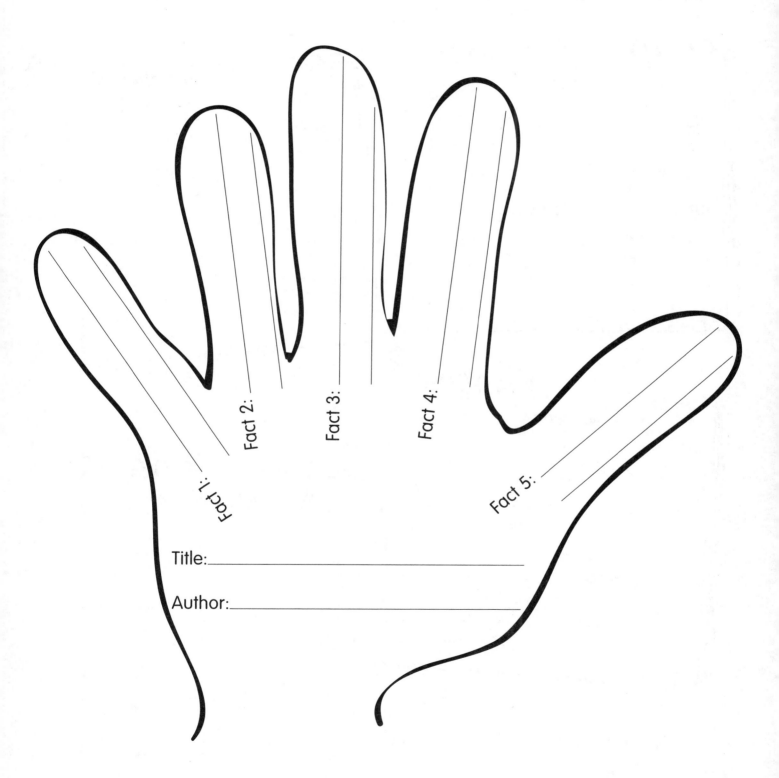

Fact 1:_____

Fact 2:_____

Fact 3:_____

Fact 4:_____

Fact 5:_____

Title:_____

Author:_____

Nonfiction Notepads

Directions: Taking notes can help you remember what you read.
Use the notepads to take notes about a nonfiction book you are reading.

Title:_____

_____

Author:_____

_____

Important Words to Know

Facts I Learned

Questions I Still Have